BABY KOALA

Published in Canada by Fitzhenry & Whiteside, 195 Allstate Parkway, Markham, Ontario L3R 4T8

Published in the United States by Fitzhenry & Whiteside, 311 Washington Street, Brighton, Massachusetts 02135

10 9 8 7 6 5 4 3 2

National Library of Canada Cataloguing in Publication
Lang, Aubrey
Baby koala / text by Aubrey Lang ; photography by Wayne Lynch.
(Nature babies)
ISBN 1-55041-874-2 (bound).—ISBN 1-55041-876-9 (pbk.)
1. Koala—Infancy—Juvenile literature. I. Lynch, Wayne
II. Title. III. Series: Lang, Aubrey. Nature babies.
QL737.M384L34 2003   599.2'5139 C2003-902551-9

U.S. Cataloging-in-Publication Data
(Library of Congress Standards)
Lang, Aubrey.
Baby koala / Aubrey Lang ; Wayne Lynch. _ 1st ed.
[36] p. : col. photos. ; cm.   (Nature babies)
Includes bibliographical references and index.
Summary: The baby koala waits until she is six months old before she emerges from her mother's pouch.
The baby isn't that curious about the outside world at first, but she's content to go along for the ride
in Mother's pouch. Later she'll ride piggyback as they search the trees for the most tender eucalyptus leaves.
But one day soon the youngster will have to face one of the greatest dangers in a koala's life—fire.
ISBN 1-55041-874-2   ISBN 1-55041-876-9 (pbk.)
1. Koalas -- Juvenile literature. (1. Koalas.) I. Lynch, Wayne. II. Title.   III. Series.
599.25 21   QL795.K62.L36 2003

Fitzhenry & Whiteside acknowledges with thanks the Canada Council for the Arts, and the Ontario Arts Council for their support of our publishing program. We acknowledge the financial support of the Government of Canada through the Book Publishing Industry Development Program (BPIDP) for our publishing activities.

ONTARIO ARTS COUNCIL
CONSEIL DES ARTS DE L'ONTARIO

Canada Council   Conseil des Arts
for the Arts   du Canada

Design by Wycliffe Smith Design Inc.
Printed in Hong Kong

BABY KOALA

Text by Aubrey Lang
Photography by Wayne Lynch

Fitzhenry & Whiteside

BEFORE YOU BEGIN

Dear Reader:

We love to watch and photograph baby animals. We wrote this book to share with you some of the adventures in the life of a koala. We photographed the koalas in this book on three different trips to Australia, which is the only place where you will find these cute, cuddly animals. Wild koalas live high up in the trees, and we often got a sore neck when we watched them for a long time. We always tried to be as quiet as possible and not disturb them.

We wish to thank Lone Pine Koala Sanctuary in Brisbane *(www.koala.net)*, especially supervisor Karen Nilsson, for their advice and assistance.

—Aubrey Lang and Wayne Lynch

TABLE OF CONTENTS

When the baby koala is born she is no bigger than a jellybean and weighs less than a penny. She looks like a tiny, pink, wiggly worm. Like a mother kangaroo, the mother koala has a pouch on her belly. The baby koala crawls inside the warm pouch and hides there for six months, drinking her mother's milk and growing big and furry.

One day she wriggles out of the pouch for the first time.

The baby koala is nervous when she first leaves the pouch. She clings like glue to her mother's thick fur. Life outside the pouch is new and interesting, and the curious baby looks around. She feels safest between her mother's front legs. When a cold wind begins to blow, she squeezes back inside the pouch to warm up.

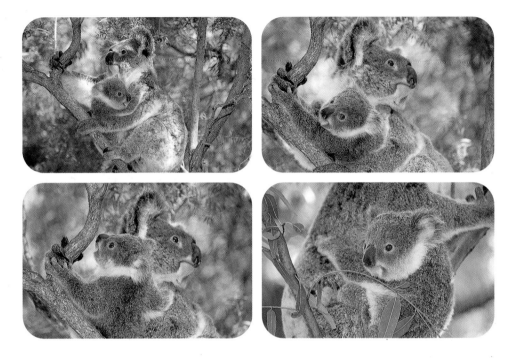

At seven months old, the baby is bigger. The young koala squirms and wiggles all the time, and she likes to grab branches and leaves. It's hard for the mother to climb with a fat baby stuck to her chest. One morning, the baby bravely climbs onto her mother's back. From now on she will only ride piggyback.

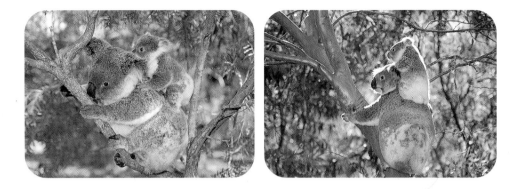

A koala has two thumbs and three fingers on each of its front feet. This gives the baby a strong grip that she will need to climb trees when she is older. Her sharp claws will help her hold onto slippery bark so that she doesn't fall and hurt herself. For now, the baby practices climbing up and down her mother's furry back.

The baby's father left before she was born. Koala fathers always live alone, and the mother raises the baby by herself.

Koalas spend most of their time in trees. If it is hot in the middle of the day, the mother moves to a shady part of the tree to keep them both cool.

Koalas have a boring diet – leaves, leaves, and more leaves. The leaves that grow on eucalyptus trees smell like cough medicine and are the koalas' favorite foods. The mother eats so many of the eucalyptus leaves that even her fur smells like medicine. The baby learns from her mother which leaves are best to eat.

photo by Brett Kullman

It has been hot and dry for many weeks. One afternoon the mother koala is awakened from her snooze by the smell of smoke. The mother and baby are in great danger. There's a fire in the forest. The baby holds on tight as her mother hurries away from the smoke and flames. They escape to another part of the forest where they are safe.

Fire is one of the biggest dangers in a koala's life, but there are other dangers too. Large eagles and owls can snatch a small koala from a mother's back. The baby is now ten months old, and she is big enough to be safe from these predators. But wild dogs, called dingoes, are still dangerous for koalas on the ground.

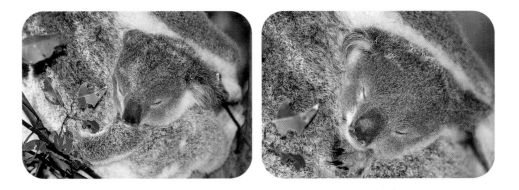

Koalas are lazybones. They sleep and sleep and sleep. They sleep twice as long as you do. When they're tired of sleeping, they sleep some more. The mother koala sleeps as much as her baby. Even when they're awake, they move around very little. Eucalyptus leaves, the most common food that koalas eat, don't give them much energy.

One day the young koala is brave enough to leave her mother's back. She grabs a large branch nearby and slowly climbs on her own. The branch is slippery and she gets scared. The young koala doesn't want to explore anymore. She whimpers and reaches out to her mother, where she will feel safe again.

Each day for the past month, the young koala has climbed farther and farther away from her mother. Now she enjoys exploring alone. She even travels to the end of thin branches where she can find juicy young leaves to eat. Such small branches would break if her mother tried to follow. The mother koala is much too heavy.

As the young koala explores the different trees in the eucalyptus forest, she meets interesting neighbors. At night the brushtail possum comes out of a hole in a hollow tree where it lives, and runs along the branches. During the day colorful squawking parrots sometimes land nearby, and the koala often watches kangaroos and spiny echidnas moving through the forest.

For several days, a large male koala has been climbing in the same trees as the young koala and her mother. The big male often points his nose to the sky and grunts loudly like a pig. He rubs branches with the smelly brown fur on his chest. The noisy male will be the father of the mother's next baby.

The mother koala now has a tiny new baby in her pouch. It's time for the young koala, who is now a year old, to leave her mother and live by herself. She stays close by because this is the area of the forest that she knows best. In another year, when she is bigger, the young koala will become a mother herself.

DID YOU KNOW?

- Adult male koalas weigh roughly twice as much as females. A large male can be the size of a small dog, and weigh up to 13.5 kilograms (30 pounds).

- Koalas are marsupials. All marsupials give birth to tiny, naked, undeveloped young that crawl into their mother's pouch and attach to a nipple. Here they nurse continuously until they are covered with fur and big enough to leave the pouch. Bears are not marsupials, so a koala should not be called a koala *bear*. The two animals are unrelated.

- The leaves of eucalyptus trees are hard to digest. Adult koalas have bacteria in their intestines that break down the tough leaves and help them get the most nutrition from their food. At five to six months of age, before the baby koala starts to chew on leaves, it eats a special kind of liquid feces from its mother, which contains the bacteria the baby needs.

- A koala is not very active. Eucalyptus leaves are not a rich source of nutrition, so a koala needs to conserve its energy. In 24 hours the average koala will spend 14.5 hours sleeping, 4.5 hours resting but awake, 4.5 hours eating, and 4 minutes traveling.

- When a koala is hot, the soles of its feet perspire. To cool off, it straddles a branch and lets its feet dangle with its toes outstretched.

- Rival males may fight over a female during the breeding season from September to December. They bite each other on the head and swat with their front claws. Sometimes they knock each other out of the tree. Injuries from these fights can be fatal.

- Normally koalas have only one baby at a time, but occasionally they have twins.

INDEX

BIOGRAPHIES

When Dr. Wayne Lynch met Aubrey Lang, he was an emergency doctor and she was a pediatric nurse. Within five years they were married and had left their jobs in medicine to work together as writers and wildlife photographers. For twenty-five years they have explored the great wilderness areas of the world – tropical rainforests, remote islands in the Arctic and Antarctic, deserts, mountains, and African grasslands.

Dr. Lynch is a popular guest lecturer and an award-winning science writer. He is the author of more than two dozen titles for adults and children. His books cover a wide range of subjects, from the biology and behavior of penguins and northern bears, arctic and grassland ecology, to the lives of prairie birds and mountain wildlife. He is a Fellow of the internationally recognized Explorers Club, and an elected Fellow of the prestigious Arctic Institute of North America.

Ms. Lang is the author of over a dozen nature books for children. She loves to share her wildlife experiences with young readers.

The couple's impressive photo credits include thousands of images published worldwide.